Angela

ELIJAH

God'...

Susan Martins Miller

**Illustrated by
Ken Save**

BARBOUR
PUBLISHING

604 285-2098

© 1991 by Barbour Publishing, Inc.

ISBN 1-58660-945-9

Published by Barbour Publishing, Inc., P.O. Box 719, Uhrichsville, Ohio 44683, www.barbourbooks.com

 Member of the
Evangelical Christian
Publishers Association

Printed in the United States of America.
5 4 3 2 1

ELIJAH

TWO WEARY TRAVELERS ARRIVED AT THE CITY LIMITS.

1

MESSAGE FROM GOD

At midday all the townspeople broke from their activities and came out into the streets to enjoy the clear sky and warm weather. Children played with their homemade toys, kicked rocks, and laughed and squealed as they chased each other from house to house. Women with squirming babies on their hips gathered in small groups to catch up on family new ways to prepare food. Men in the shops looked out at their families and smiled with satisfaction at the comfortable life they were living. No one paid any attention to the two weary travelers as they arrived at the city limits.

The day had been very warm, and the sun was at its peak. Elijah the prophet, accompanied by his companion and servant, had been walking for several hours. Now they had reached their destination: Samaria, where the king lived. They had stopped at the outskirts of the city to draw water from a well to quench their thirst and wash the day's dust from their faces and arms. In only a few more minutes they would arrive at the palace and meet with King Ahab and Queen Jezebel.

"Don't be nervous, Reuben," Elijah said to his young servant, who was swallowing hard and sweating more than usual. "We're doing what the Lord has asked us to do; everything will be fine."

He smiled at Reuben, trying to help him relax.

"Master, you have told me what you are going to say to the king, and I do not think he is going to like it. I fear for your safety." The younger man was very devoted to the prophet for whom he had been working for several years. He always had a hard time understanding how Elijah stayed so calm.

"Thank you, Reuben. We will both be fine." Now they had arrived at the king's residence. Days earlier they had sent a messenger ahead to confirm that King Ahab would see them when they arrived. The enormous carved gates, heavy with gold trim, swung open, and the two men were ushered into the king's private courtyard. A servant offered them a cool drink and left them to wait for the royal couple.

Reuben slowly walked in a circle, looking in all directions at the ornate carvings and lush

"MASTER, THIS IS A BREATHTAKING PLACE!"

garden plants surrounding them. "Master, this is a breathtaking place!"

"Yes, it is even more beautiful than I had heard." Elijah also was taking in every detail of the courtyard and admiring the tasteful arrangements of statues and fountains.

Their thoughts were interrupted by the king's servant returning to announce that the king was ready to speak to them. King Ahab entered the courtyard through a large doorway. Queen Jezebel followed a few steps behind. Elijah had asked only to speak with the king, but she was anxious to meet the prophet Elijah and wondered what he would have to say to her husband.

"Elijah, I am very pleased to have you come to see me." The king seemed in a friendly mood. "Why have you not come sooner?"

Elijah bowed his head to the king. "Thank

QUEEN JEZEBEL LOOKED ALARMED NOW.

you, King Ahab. I am a servant of the Lord, and I follow His leading. I am here now because God has sent me to you." The king was still smiling, but Elijah could not help noticing that Queen Jezebel looked alarmed now. He had heard that she had a great deal of influence on the king, and he could see that this was true.

"Am I to be honored by receiving a message from God?" Ahab was excited, but Jezebel was even more disturbed by her husband's enthusiasm.

"King Ahab, you also are a servant of the Lord. He has given you a great responsibility to rule over the people of Israel. He has given me a message for you so that you may be a better king for His people."

"I am already a very powerful king, Elijah. What are you getting at?" The smile was gone from Ahab's face, and he was getting impatient.

"The Lord is not pleased with all that you have done, my king." Elijah did not dare stop to take a breath, or the king would not let him finish speaking. "You have been very wicked in your actions, and you have allowed Queen Jezebel to deceive you into believing you ought to worship a false god instead of the one true God. The Lord wants you to stop worshiping Baal and help the people to follow the true God. You must destroy—"

Jezebel interrupted Elijah's speech with angry words of her own. "Ahab, surely you are not going to allow this man to speak to you this way! You are the king, and he is insulting both of us!"

"Jezebel is right," Ahab snapped at Elijah. "I am the king, after all. You have no right to tell me what to do or to accuse the queen of doing anything wrong. Don't you realize you

"THE LORD WANTS YOU TO STOP WORSHIPING BAAL."

are risking your life by speaking to me this way? Being a prophet does not entitle you to be disrespectful."

"I do not mean to be disrespectful, my king. You yourself have said that I am a prophet. Surely you know I must speak God's message, whatever it is."

Ahab walked across the courtyard and stood next to Jezebel. "I have not stopped worshiping the God of Israel. But Baal also is a god who must be pleased. The people are free to worship as they choose."

Elijah swallowed and took a moment to pray and collect his thoughts. He knew he must obey the Lord, but obviously Ahab was not going to change his mind. "I have spoken the message of the Lord, my king. You say you believe in God. If you do, hear His words and change your ways."

"Elijah, I was flattered you came to see me, but now I am getting angry." Ahab's face was already turning red.

"My king, because you have disobeyed the Lord, there will be drought and famine for several years. You teach that Baal is lord of the rain clouds, but you will see that he is powerless to give rain. There will be no rain except at my word, King Ahab."

Ahab and Jezebel were both outraged at this prophecy of a drought. In a vicious, loud voice, Ahab ordered his servants to make sure that Elijah and Reuben left the city immediately. Reuben became frightened that the king would try to kill them and was glad to get out of the courtyard alive. He pleaded with his master to leave Samaria as quickly as possible. Elijah knew the danger they faced but assured Reuben that the Lord would lead them to a safe place.

"YOU MUST REPENT, KING AHAB."

The traveled east and across the Jordan River and found a dry place in a ravine. Elijah seemed to know exactly where to go, and Reuben wanted to be as far from Ahab as possible. As they settled down at the end of the second day, he began to wonder what they were going to eat. They had traveled far beyond any marketplace without buying food. However, he had learned from serving Elijah all these years not to question the prophet's judgment. As darkness fell, he laid out their bedrolls on the softest place he could find.

It was barely dawn when Reuben was awaked by a gentle flapping of bird wings. He looked up and saw a group of jet-black ravens descending on them. Something was different about these birds—they were carrying something. They landed in a circle at the foot of his mat and released their cargo. Reuben was astonished to

A GROUP OF JET-BLACK RAVENS
DESCENDED ON THEM.

discover they had been carrying meat and bread—enough for the two men to have a hearty breakfast. He turned excitedly to wake Elijah but found the prophet already awake and smiling.

"Yes, Reuben, I knew they would come," Elijah said. "The Lord has sent them with food, and there is a brook just over there. We will be well taken care of while we are here."

2

Flour and Oil

Day after day the ravens came, in the morning and again in the evening. Elijah and Reuben were never hungry, and water from the brook brought them cool refreshment from their thirst. They enjoyed these weeks of quiet companionship and gave thanks each day for the way God was caring for them. Nevertheless, they could not help noticing that the heat was intensifying and, as Elijah had predicted, there was no rain. Eventually the brook which had been so bountiful when they arrived became more shallow and flowed more slowly. The mud on the bottom was turning to dry dirt. The two men began to ration their supply very carefully each day, but it was clear that they would soon have to leave this place of refuge.

Each day Elijah would wander off by himself to pray and listen for God's voice to tell them where they should go next. One day he returned to Reuben and said simply, "Zarephath, near Sidon."

Reuben was taken aback. Sidon was in the very heart of the territory from which Baal worship had come and was a place where Queen Jezebel's own father was very powerful. No one in that region would welcome a prophet like Elijah. Most of the people were not even

21

Israelites. Reuben was reluctant to leave the safety of the ravine for a long and tiring trip into a dangerous area. He took comfort in knowing that Elijah wanted to do what God asked him to do, even as Reuben himself wanted to please his master, Elijah.

So they crossed back over the Jordan and walked west to the coast and then turned north. As they made their way slowly up the coast toward Zarephath, they saw the effect of the drought everywhere. By this time it was obvious that the crops would fail, and theirs was not the only brook which had dried up. Everyone was hoarding food for their own families, leaving strangers to fend for themselves. As they journeyed, God provided for them each day, but they began to sense the desperation which gripped the people.

At last the day came that they arrived in

Zarephath. Elijah had heard from the Lord what was to happen and began to search the faces of people they encountered. He was looking for the one woman through whom God would work. At the outskirts of the city he found a woman gathering dry sticks to fuel her fire at home. She was with a group of friends yet kept to herself away from them. She seemed to always slump, never fully standing up after picking up a stick. The prophet recognized her as the one whom God meant for him to meet. He felt a familiar pressure in his mind which said, without words, "Yes, she is the one. Speak to her."

Elijah approached the woman, who was young but had a mournful expression which made her look older. He said, "I have been traveling for many days, and it has been a long time since we passed a well. If you live nearby, may I

HE FOUND A WOMAN GATHERING DRY STICKS.

trouble you for a jar of water?"

The woman's friends stopped their chattering and protectively moved closer to her. "Come on, Leah," one of them said. "It's time to go home."

Leah looked from Elijah to her friends. "All he wants is some water." To Elijah she said, "I can come back in a few minutes with a jar of water for you and your friend. It's much too hot today to deny you a drink of water." She turned to follow after her friends on the road into town.

"And would you also please bring me some bread?" Elijah's request made the whole group freeze in their footsteps and turn and stare. Didn't this stranger know there was a famine? None of them had any extra food, least of all Leah, a widow with no family except a young son, whom she was already struggling to feed.

"ALL HE WANTS IS SOME WATER."

How could this man so rudely ask her for bread?

Leah lowered her head and closed her eyes for a moment. She turned back to Elijah and spoke in a muffled voice. "I can see that you are an Israelite, and I have heard many things about your God. As surely as the Lord your God lives, I don't have any bread. I have only a handful of flour in a jar and a little oil." She began to choke on her words and could hardly talk. "I am taking these sticks home to make a meal for my son, and I will eat what is left. But I am afraid it will be our last meal. As hard as I have tried, I cannot find more food anywhere. We are surely going to starve! No, I cannot bring you bread." Her whole body sagged with sadness as she once again began to walk home.

Elijah quickly reached out and put his hand on her shoulder. Even the looseness of her garment did not hide the bony thinness of her form. "Don't be afraid," he said very quietly. "I do not mean to cause hardship for you."

She looked at him through tears which she could no longer hold back. "Don't ask me to choose between feeding you—a stranger—and feeding my own son."

"Leah, the man's an idiot. Come with us right now." Her friend was pulling forcefully on her elbow, almost causing her to stumble.

Elijah continued in a steady tone. "Of course you must feed your son. You are his mother; he depends on you. Go home and make the meal you have planned. But first make me just a small cake of bread and bring it back here."

"Sir, I cannot help you! I have no food!" How could he ask again after she had explained that she herself faced starvation? How could she make him understand? Maybe he really was a lunatic and not just a thirsty traveler.

ELIJAH CONTINUED IN A STEADY TONE.

Elijah held her firmly by the shoulders and looked her straight in the face as he spoke loudly enough for everyone to hear. "The Lord, the God of Israel, has said that your jar of flour and your jug of oil will not be used up until the day that the Lord gives rain to the land once again."

"Who are you?" Leah was not being sarcastic. She probed his face in a genuine desire to know why he could so confidently make such an outrageous statement. "I have heard that a man of God in Israel has cursed the land and brought this drought on all of us. Are you that man?"

"God is the only one who has the power to stop the rain. I am only His messenger, and I have given you His message. Will you bring me some bread?"

Leah looked again at her friends. They were obviously astounded at what Elijah was asking

SHE DID NOT KNOW WHAT TO DO.

of her and murmured among themselves about what she should do. Leah did not owe this stranger anything, they said. What he was saying made no sense at all. They urged her to go home to her son and forget she had even met him.

When she looked at Elijah, Leah saw a confidence and peace which she and her friends lacked. He really believed what he had said to her, as ridiculous as it sounded. She knew that the Israelites claimed that their God was very powerful. If He were powerful enough to stop the rain, perhaps He could really keep her food from running out.

She felt like a statue of stone, standing absolutely still because she did not know what to do.

3

THE MIRACLE

"Leah, I absolutely forbid you to do this!" After hearing about her meeting with Elijah, Leah's mother-in-law had come running down the village street to her small house, holding the hem of her garment in her hand so her feet could move more freely. "I will not permit you to give away my grandson's food!"

Leah was very determined. Without responding, she poured into a bowl the last of the

SHE POURED INTO A BOWL
THE LAST OF HER FLOUR AND OIL.

flour and oil and used her fingers to work the mixture into a smooth ball that she divided into two cakes. She patted these flat and laid them on a dish then leaned over to see if the oven was hot enough to cook them. She added two of the sticks she had just gathered. All the while the other woman was screaming at her about her foolishness and stupidity.

Her mother-in-law was getting impatient with Leah's silence. "Answer me!" she demanded loudly.

The younger woman sighed quietly and wiped her hands on a cloth. "I do not wish to speak disrespectfully to you, but I have made up my mind. I am going to bake this bread and then take it to Elijah with a jug of water."

"How can you do this? I have no more food to share with you, or my own family will go hungry."

"ANSWER ME!"

"I am not asking you to share your food. Elijah says that his God will provide for me." Leah continued her preparations.

"And you believe that?" The older woman was outraged.

Leah stopped to look directly at her relative. She raised her eyebrows and said, "Baal has not provided for me. He does not give us rain. Baal seems content to let Hiram and me starve. Why should I not turn to Elijah's God?"

"Well, I will not stand here and watch you do this." Her mother-in-law stomped out of the house, convinced that Leah had lost her mind. Leah was glad to see her go. She wished everyone would just quit treating her like a child and let her make her own decisions. She poured a jug of water and sat down to wait for the bread to bake. Her stomach fluttered with nervousness and excitement. Despite her confident words to her mother-in-law, she was not sure she was doing the right thing.

Elijah and Reuben waited patiently at the outskirts of the town. Reuben's stomach was grumbling, and after a long silence, he asked if perhaps he should go into town looking for food. His master quickly insisted that they both remain where they were to wait for Leah to return. She had not told them she would bring food, but she had promised at least water, and Elijah was determined to pray and wait.

When she did come, she was not alone. A little boy, looking thin and tired, was holding her hand, and behind them were several people gesturing wildly and calling for her to turn around and go home. Without hesitation she walked directly to Elijah and unfolded the cloths she carried to reveal the steaming bread cakes.

Elijah smiled and took them gratefully from

"YOU HAVE DONE THE RIGHT THING, LEAH."

her and set them down. He held Leah's hands in his own and said comfortingly, "You have done the right thing, Leah. It took great courage and faith to bring the last of your food to me. What I said earlier is true—you will have plenty to eat for you and your son." He stroked the small boy's head and noticed his puzzled expression. "Don't worry, Hiram. I am not stealing your supper. Your mother has more flour and oil, and she will prepare a delicious meal for the two of you."

Leah looked down at her son, wanting desperately to believe that what Elijah said was true. For her son's sake, she tried to sound confident. "Yes, Hiram. Let's go home while the oven is still hot and see what we can make for ourselves. Would you like to help?"

Hiram nodded silently, and they started to go. Suddenly Hiram said, "Look, Mother, our neighbors!"

"LET'S GO HOME WHILE THE OVEN IS STILL HOT."

The friends with whom Leah had been gathering wood were hurrying toward her now and frantically calling her name. "Leah! Leah! It's true! We went in your house looking for you to try to stop you from coming, and we saw your jars. They are full of flour and oil! You and Hiram have plenty of food."

Another friend was not so convinced. "Is this a trick?" she asked. "Have you been hiding a food supply just so you could pull a stunt like this?"

Leah turned tearfully back to Elijah. "How can I thank you? You have saved my son's life and my own. I can never repay you."

"Pay no attention to your neighbors, Leah. You have seen that the God of Israel is powerful and loving enough to provide for you. You must thank Him, not me."

"May I come back to learn more about your

God? I would like Hiram to know this God who is more powerful than Baal."

Surrounded by her bewildered friends and neighbors, Leah returned to her home and found enough flour and oil to make a hearty dinner. Despite their excitement, she insisted that her neighbors leave her to eat in peace with her son. As they waited for the bread to bake, she explained what had happened earlier in the day when she first met Elijah. Hiram had many questions which she could not answer, but she promised they would ask Elijah as soon as possible. As she tucked him into bed later, she found herself praying to this new God and feeling calmer than she had in many years. She had been very lonely since her husband died, and she had lost faith in Baal, who seemed a very distant god. This God of Israel was much nearer, she thought.

LEAH FOUND ENOUGH FLOUR AND OIL FOR A
HEARTY DINNER.

In the morning the jars again contained enough flour and oil for the day's food. She got up early and made a meal for Elijah and Reuben. She had eagerly offered the room on her roof for them to stay in while in Zarephath. If Elijah were close by, she could ask him many questions.

There was more food the next day, and again the day after that. Each day Leah gave thanks to God and took a basket of food and water to Elijah. And although this miracle of the jars never running out repeated itself every day for many months during the drought, Leah never took it for granted and each day reminded Hiram that the God of Israel was caring for them.

Every afternoon Leah would take Hiram by the hand, and they would walk up the stairs to the room where Elijah was staying. He would welcome them and invite them to sit with him. Leah and Hiram had so many questions, and Elijah patiently answered their questions and taught them about Israel's God. Leah wanted Hiram to grow up knowing the love and power of this God. Many days she was so reluctant to leave Elijah that she would go downstairs only when Hiram wailed loudly that he was hungry, and she was reminded that she must care for his body as well as his soul.

One afternoon Leah came alone. "Hiram is not feeling well," she explained. "I cannot stay to talk today, but I wanted to bring your food. I am sure he will be better tomorrow, and we will come again."

Leah left to go care for Hiram. As Elijah watched her descend the stairs standing straight and tall, he remembered how sad and slumped she had been when he first met her.

ELIJAH TAUGHT THEM ABOUT ISRAEL'S GOD.

When she was out of sight, the voice in his head whispered that this was no ordinary illness that Hiram faced.

4

DEATH TO LIFE

When it was time for their evening meal, Hiram seemed worse, not better. He was too sick to eat. Leah put her hands to his scorching skin and became frightened: The child had never been this hot before. She forced herself to stay calm and think logically about what to do. Hiram was sleeping deeply—too deeply, she thought. The bucket of water which had been at his bedside all day needed to be refilled. Leah hated to leave him for even a moment, but she went into the other room and ladled water from the large jug into the bucket. Taking a fresh cloth she returned to Hiram and once again tried to cool his body by sponging him off.

"Leah, are you home?" Her neighbor had come to see if Hiram was any better.

"He's getting worse by the minute," the desperate young mother sobbed. "What am I going to do? His fever will not come down. It's all happening so fast!"

"I'm going for the doctor," the neighbor said. "You stay here and try to keep calm. I'll be right back."

It was nearly an hour before her friend came back with the doctor. Leah sat there soundlessly watching the sun move toward the horizon. At last the doctor came in and quickly examined Hiram, who did not stir at all. "Has he been like this long?" he asked.

"No, not too long. When I went to Elijah with his food, Hiram was feeling sleepy and had a headache. I thought perhaps he'd had too much sun, so I left him here. But he's getting worse all the time. Please help my child!" Leah was terrified of what the doctor might say.

"You've done the right thing to try to cool him off and make him comfortable, Leah. I'll give you a mixture to give him. You'll have to see if you can wake him up. I'll come back in the morning, or you can send for me during the night if you need to."

"What's wrong with him, doctor?" Leah asked urgently.

"I'm not sure I can say. There have been several other children who have been very ill, but this medicine seems to help. Just be sure he takes it."

The doctor left, and Leah was once again alone with her sleeping child. She called his name, put more cool water on his face, and loosened his bedclothes. At last he began to wake up. She quickly poured the medicine into his mouth. Hiram screwed up his face at the sour taste, which made Leah smile through her tears. He did not stay awake long, but at least he had taken the medicine.

The night was long and dark. The moon was covered over by clouds, and Leah had only the light of a small candle to keep her company as she sat at Hiram's bedside. She stroked his face and smoothed his hair and prayed to the new God about whom Elijah had been teaching her. Surely this powerful God could heal her son. She wondered if Elijah could help; perhaps his prayers would be more effective. It was in the early hours of the morning that the candle

SURELY THIS POWERFUL GOD COULD HEAL HER SON.

finally flickered out. Leah did not light another one; it would be dawn soon. Out of sheer exhaustion she finally allowed herself to doze off for a few minutes.

She awoke with a start when Hiram started groaning. Immediately she reached for the medicine and carefully put some in his mouth. This time he did not even have the energy to make a face at the taste. He slumped back in his bed, and Leah suddenly realized that he was unconscious, not just sleeping. Gathering him in her arms, she tried to wake him. "Hiram! Hiram! Wake up!" But there was no response.

Leah looked out the window; it was light now. Frantically she wrapped Hiram in a blanket and went running to the house next door. "Get the doctor! Get the doctor!" she screamed. The doors and windows swung open, and her neighbor hurried toward the center of town.

The doctor came quickly; his worst fears had come true, and his examination confirmed what he thought. Hiram was not going to get well. He tried to break the news to Leah as gently as possible. He had no medicine which would help the boy now, but perhaps Hiram would feel comforted if she stayed with him.

Leah crumpled into a sobbing heap. "No! No!" she cried. "Why should Hiram be spared of starvation only to die like this?"

The doctor simply shook his head and said, "I am helpless. There is nothing I can do."

By now friends and relatives up and down the street had heard about Hiram's illness and what the doctor said. The gathering at Leah's house was in a frenzy. Some began to pray to Baal and plead for Hiram's life. Others told Leah to let the child die in peace; it must be Baal's will. Leah was horrified by the wildness which had taken over her home. She closed herself off alone with Hiram and cried inconsolably.

Suddenly she realized that Hiram was no longer breathing. She clutched her arms around him and shook him, trying to make him breathe and wake up. But it was no use. His lifeless body drooped in her arms unresponsively. As she rocked and sobbed her grief turned to anger. *Elijah,* she thought. *Elijah has done this!*

At that moment Elijah came into the room. "You!" she cried. "Why are you doing this to me? You have taught me about your loving God, and I even believed you. God is punishing me. If you were not living in my house, I would not know of your God, and He would pay no attention to me. He would not be punishing me for my sin."

Elijah stood silently for several minutes. At last he spoke. "Leah, you are asking why the

God who promised life is bringing death instead. This is not an easy question, and I have no easy answers. Let me take Hiram upstairs and ask our God for answers."

"You have done enough, Elijah!" Leah shouted. She gripped Hiram's body even tighter and began to sob again.

Elijah crossed the room and stood next to her. Gently he pried her arms loose and put his own around the boy. He cradled Hiram tenderly and made his way up the stairs to his room on the roof. With a heavy heart he laid the child out on his own bed.

He began to pray out loud. "O Lord my God, is it because I am staying with this widow that you have brought tragedy to her? Have you let her son die? She has come so far in believing in you. Is this how it will end?"

The prophet, praying continuously, stretched

"LET ME TAKE HIRAM UPSTAIRS."

himself out on top of Hiram. He cried to the Lord, "Let this boy's life return to him!" He stood up and waited, but nothing happened. Once again he stretched out over Hiram, warming the body which had begun to grow cold. "O Lord my God, give Leah back her son!" Again there was no response. Elijah hung his head and began to cry himself. He could not believe that Hiram was gone—that sweet child who came up the stairs every day to learn about God.

A third time he stretched himself out on Hiram and pleaded with God. "Give this boy back his life, mighty God. Death is nothing to you, the Giver of Life."

Elijah quickly rolled off the bed when he felt the boy's chest begin to heave. Hiram was coughing and groaning—but he was alive! He was breathing! The grateful man cradled him once more and gave thanks to God. Before he got all the way down the stairs, Hiram lifted his head off of Elijah's shoulder to look around and wonder what all the fuss was about.

Leah reached out her arms to take her son. Elijah said simply, "Look, your son is alive!"

"I know I doubted you and said awful things to you," Leah began. "Once again I don't know how I can thank you for giving life to my son."

"And once again I must remind you that it is God who gives life."

The young widow choked back her tears and declared confidently, "You are truly a man of God!"

HE WAS ALIVE! HE WAS BREATHING!

5

Meeting with the King

Elijah finally gave up trying to sleep. Turning his head to the east, he saw the faint glimmer of the sun oozing across the horizon at last. He had been awake most of the night, fighting off what he knew was true: It was time to arrange a meeting with King Ahab. After leaving Zarephath, Elijah and Reuben had traveled east and south again. When they heard reports that Ahab was looking for them, they kept moving

"THIS IS THE DAY WE WILL FIND AHAB."

to keep out of his way. But now it had been three long years since the drought began, and everywhere they went, people of all ages were running out of food. The crops could not grow; the pastures had turned into hard, dry dirt which cracked in the heat; buckets lowered into the wells came up empty. The time had come for a showdown.

With every muscle in his body aching, Elijah pulled himself up off the ground and rolled his bedding. He had heard reports that the king's pastures could no longer support his horses and mules, and Ahab was in search of new land. Elijah had been avoiding Ahab for so long, but now the Lord was urging him to confront the king and surely would lead his steps. Gathering up the few things he kept with him, Elijah nudged his servant and roused him from a sound sleep. "Come on, Reuben," he said gently. "The Lord has another task for us."

THE TALL YOUNG VISITOR SLOWED HIS PACE.

"Master, it's still very dark. Shouldn't we wait for daylight?"

"No, Reuben. I think this is the day we will find Ahab. There's no point in putting it off."

"How will we know where to go?"

Elijah shrugged. "How do we ever know where to go? The Lord will lead us. I think we should head closer to Samaria."

The young servant hoisted their bundles over his shoulder, and the two men walked until midday. It was a quiet road, and they encountered few people as they progressed toward Samaria. When the sun was high in the sky, they sought shade under a shriveling tree, its branches bare and thirsty. They had little to eat besides bread cakes, but their appetites were subdued by the foreboding feeling that the day would not end as quietly as it had begun. After eating a few bites, Elijah stretched out for a few minutes of sleep;

the long, wakeful night was taking its toll.

Suddenly his eyes snapped open. He had sensed the oncoming presence of someone walking quickly toward them. The tall young visitor slowed his pace as he approached the travelers. Soon he was close enough to cast a shadow over the place where they sat.

"You are Obadiah, the king's servant," Elijah said quietly.

"Yes, I am! I thought I recognized you— you are Elijah, aren't you?"

"Yes, I have come to see Ahab. Is he with you?"

Obadiah looked over his shoulder. "We went in opposite directions looking for pasture land. Of course, there is none to be found."

"Obadiah, I want you to find Ahab and tell him I want to speak to him."

The color drained from Obadiah's face, and

"THE KING WANTS TO KILL YOU!"

his brown eyes grew big. With a gasp, he said, "But Elijah, the king wants to kill you! He's been looking for you all over the country. I've been secretly hiding other prophets—I could protect you, too."

"No, I must see Ahab. Today, Obadiah."

"But if he knows I spoke to you—it could be dangerous for me. What if he doesn't find you when he comes back this way? He'll kill me!"

"I give you my word, Obadiah, I'm not going anywhere." Elijah spoke steadily and patiently. He put his hand on Obadiah's shoulder and felt the fear in the young man's body. "Do you think you can find the king for me?"

"I will try, Elijah, if this is the Lord's will."

Neither Reuben nor Elijah wanted more to eat after Obadiah left. They put away their uneaten food and sat in silence. Elijah prayed for courage and boldness to speak to Ahab with

God's message. He knew that his life was in great peril.

Dusk had begun to fall when Reuben spotted the cloud of dust moving toward them. It was the king and his servants traveling rapidly down the road and kicking up the dry dirt. Even at a distance, Elijah could see the rage in Ahab's walk. He did not call out. As Ahab got closer, the two stared at each other without words. When they were face-to-face, no one dared move a muscle. Reuben and the king's servants waited tensely for one of the leaders to speak.

Finally Ahab spat in the dirt at his feet and angrily demanded water. One of his servants immediately brought him a cup, and Ahab poured it down his throat in one gulp.

"Elijah, you know I've been hunting you. Your days are numbered, I'll see to that!"

"Ahab, I only do what the Lord tells me to

NO ONE DARED MOVE A MUSCLE.

do, you know that."

Ahab waved his arm and spun around on one heel. "Look at this! So many people are suffering because of your self-centered stubbornness. Call off this ridiculous curse and let it rain! Why do you insist on causing trouble for all of Israel with your silly prophecies?"

"Are my words really so silly, Ahab?" Elijah asked, unafraid. "I have not cursed this land; God has done this—and it is because of your disobedience and refusal to follow his commands."

"Your God is not the only god, Elijah. There is Baal to think of. He is powerful and vengeful."

"If you really believe that, let us put it to the test." Elijah's words were coming fast now. It was his voice speaking, but the Lord's message was being spoken. "Meet me on Mount Carmel. Bring four hundred and fifty prophets of Baal with you. You can even bring four hundred

SHOULD AHAB, KING OF ALL ISRAEL, BE AFRAID?

prophets of Asherah, the god whom Jezebel is so fond of. We will see how powerful they are."

"And who will you bring?" Ahab asked. He was sure there was a trick in Elijah's words.

"I bring with me the power of the true God." Elijah's voice was strong and confident, and he looked Ahab straight in the eye. "Call the people from all over Israel, Ahab. Let them see for themselves and decide who is causing trouble."

Ahab's face was bright red, and sweat was dripping from his forehead. He looked at Elijah and Reuben, two poor and rootless men who traveled the countryside saying ridiculous things. Why should he, Ahab, king of all Israel, be afraid of them? Yet he was. He knew he must not let his servants see his fear.

"I don't know why I don't kill you both on the spot," he said viciously. "I'll play your little game, but you'd better be careful!"

6

MOUNT CARMEL

The king's household was in a furious uproar. Ahab shouted orders to his advisors then changed his mind and threatened to punish them for no reason. The servants were afraid to do anything at all for fear of making him angry. He demanded that all his advisors be present and snapped at them because they did not know what he wanted without being told. His children

peered out from behind the pillars of the courtyard and wondered what had made their father
so upset. All the food which had been prepared
for his homecoming had been untouched. If the
king did not want to eat, no one else dared to
eat either.

Jezebel was running after Ahab, following on
his heels everywhere he went. If he crossed to the
other side of the courtyard, she was right behind
him. If he sat down, she sat down beside him.
Those watching could see her gesturing wildly
and angrily, and before long their whispered argu-
ment became loud enough for everyone to hear.

"What a coward you are, Ahab! How could
you let him speak to you that way?" she shouted.

"You weren't there, Jezebel. You don't know
what it was like—all those people watching me
and that silly old man being so calm about the
whole thing."

JEZEBEL WAS RUNNING AFTER AHAB.

"You should have just killed him right there, Ahab. You were a fool not to."

"I couldn't do that, woman! If you don't leave me alone, perhaps that is what I will do to you!" he threatened.

"You haven't got the courage; we both know that." Clearly Jezebel was not afraid of her husband. They sat for a few moments in silence, trying to decide what their next move should be.

"So what do you think I should do?" Ahab finally asked.

Jezebel had her answer ready. "Everything you do from now on must discredit Elijah. Go to the people and make him look like the fool that you know he is. Meet him on Mount Carmel—you can't get out of that—but be prepared to throw him to the dogs."

"Of course you are right, as always, Jezebel." Ahab sighed wearily. "Why should a king have

AHAB CALLED HIS CLOSEST ADVISORS.

to prove himself this way?" He picked up a piece of bread from the plate which had been set beside him several hours ago. The famine had touched even the king's household, and nothing which had been presented to him to eat looked very good. "We must go to work."

Ahab called his closest advisors to gather around him. They must come up with a clear plan of action, he told them. It was important to maintain control of the situation. Elijah must not be allowed to get the upper hand in the opinion of the people. They must be prepared for whatever might happen on Mount Carmel. Cautiously, the advisors began to make suggestions.

"We must divide the nation into territories and send messengers to the people," one suggested. "Elijah does not have people working for him like you do, my king. You have the obvious advantage of reaching the people first."

Another suggested that the king make threats against groups of people unless they appeared on Mount Carmel and sided with Ahab. A third recommended that the messengers going to the people make statements about Elijah which would make him seem like a foolish old man. Certainly the people would side with Ahab then.

Soon the courtyard was alive with activity. Maps were spread out on the ground; lists were made of the young men who ran the fastest—these would serve as messengers for the king. A scribe took down ideas and information which could be used to turn the people against Elijah. Even Jezebel sat back and smiled with pleasure at the scheming and deceit brewing in her household. Ahab just needed a gentle push, she told herself, and he could seem smarter and braver than he really was. She watched with delight as he moved from group to group,

JEZEBEL SMILED AT THE SCHEMING AND DECEIT.

overseeing the plans being made.

However, a dark cloud hung over the entire gathering: What did Elijah really want? What was really going to happen on Mount Carmel? How could they possibly be prepared for it? The king's advisors tried their best to guess what Elijah was planning, but they knew they could not be sure until the day arrived. Therefore it was crucial that they reach the people with Ahab's message before Elijah had a chance to mislead them with words of his own.

At the outskirts of town, Reuben expressed his astonishment at what Elijah was proposing to do. "Master!" he exclaimed. "How can we challenge the king like this? He has dozens of advisors and hundreds of servants and can order anyone to do his will. What can possibly happen on Mount Carmel to make the people more afraid of you than they are of their king?"

"GOD IS THE ONE CHALLENGING AHAB."

Elijah shook his head and sighed. "Reuben, my friend, you have been with me for a long time. Haven't you seen the power of God displayed enough times to know that the Lord will not fail in this effort? God is the one challenging Ahab, not us."

"But, master—surely we ought to prepare in some way."

"Yes, you are right about that. And we will, first thing in the morning. For now, let's get some sleep."

Elijah slept soundly as Reuben tossed and turned. He swatted at the bugs swarming around his neck and wished that he had not let the campfire burn out. It seemed impossible to even think about sleeping. Suddenly he sat up very straight; he was sure he had heard footsteps in the dark. He peered into the night, looking for any hint of a shadow in the moonlight. He

SUDDENLY HE SAT UP VERY STRAIGHT.

gasped as a figure emerged from the bushes and then sighed with relief as he realized it was Obadiah. He whispered rapidly to the visitor, asking what in the world he was doing coming to them in the middle of the night.

Though they continued to speak in hushed voices, Elijah was soon awake and joined in the conversation. Obadiah offered to help Elijah however he could and reminded the prophet of the devout followers of God whom he had been hiding in caves during the famine so that Ahab and Jezebel could not kill them. These men could now act as Elijah's messengers, he suggested, and he himself would be able to find out about Ahab's plans and report them to Elijah.

Obadiah was gone before daylight, and by the middle of the morning their plans were put into effect. Other believers who had been hiding from Ahab now knew that God would protect them.

Sensing the significance of Elijah's challenge to the king, they traveled the roads of the countryside talking to the people in the towns and villages and calling them to go to Mount Carmel and see for themselves the power of God.

At first it seemed their efforts were fruitless. It seemed that if anyone was planning to go to Mount Carmel, it was because they were frightened into it by Ahab's threats. Late one night, Obadiah and several leaders met with Elijah in a closed room and shared their discouragement.

"The king is still the king, Elijah," they said, "and the people are afraid of him. Only a few are really planning to make the trip—relatives of the priests of Baal, mostly. Provisions for a journey like this are too hard to come by. There won't be many on your side." They shook their heads in exasperation at the situation.

"It is not my side we are talking about," Elijah

"I AM NOT CONCERNED FOR MYSELF."

said. "I am grateful for the effort you all are making, but you still don't seem to understand. I am not concerned for myself. It is God who will be victorious on Mount Carmel in a few days. You must tell the people that they are not making a choice between Ahab and Elijah, as the king would have them believe, but between Baal and God."

The messengers went out once more, returning to some of the same villages and finding others who had not yet heard the news of the challenge. Gradually they began to see some progress. Here and there a family was strapping supplies to the back of a mule: blankets, the last of their flour and oil, empty jugs in case they should find water on the way. Many things they needed were not to be found; they would have to scrounge for them as they traveled. Soon it was certain that there would be thousands of

A FAMILY WAS STRAPPING SUPPLIES
TO THE BACK OF A MULE.

people on the mountain.

Elijah and those who had rallied around him began to make their own preparations for traveling. Elijah and Reuben traveled with few provisions, as always, but they would not walk the road alone this time. As their departure grew near, Elijah called Obadiah aside and asked for one last preparation: two bulls. Healthy animals were hard to find and Obadiah could hardly keep himself from asking for more explanation, but he did as Elijah asked. In the early hours of a morning just a few weeks after their roadside encounter, Obadiah and Elijah led the group of believers on the road toward Mount Carmel.

OBADIAH AND ELIJAH LED
THE GROUP OF BELIEVERS.

7

The Lord Is Faithful

Makeshift tents and tattered bedrolls covered all the clear spots on the mountainside. Any place that was fairly level had become the temporary home of a family which had made the journey to Mount Carmel. There was a whispered rumor making its way from campfire to campfire that the water supply on the mountain had not yet dried up completely. Mothers loaded their young

AHAB ESTABLISHED HIS HEADQUARTERS.

children with water jugs and sent them off in search of this precious liquid.

The people watched with anticipation and excitement as Ahab established his headquarters at the top of the mountain. He had brought with him four hundred and fifty prophets of Baal and four hundred prophets of Asherah, along with his own advisors and servants. Over a thousand people were bustling around trying to be sure the king was happy. Elijah and his followers, numbering only a few dozen, quietly settled in among the people.

Late in the day Elijah climbed to a high place where he could be seen by all of the people. A hush went over the crowd as he began to speak.

"You are the people of Israel, children of the one true God. God our Father has been faithful to us. He brought our forefathers out of the

"WE HAVE DISOBEYED HIM
AND TURNED TO OTHER GODS."

land of Egypt and into the Promised Land. Yet we have disobeyed Him and turned to other gods. We have not taught our children about the true God who alone is powerful.

"Now our land is filled with altars to Baal and Asherah, and the altars which our forefathers built have fallen in ruins. The people say that they still believe in Israel's God, but they also accept Baal as their god.

"How long will you continue to do this? You cannot serve two gods! If the Lord is God, then follow Him. But if Baal is God, follow Baal. What will you do?"

The people began to murmur among themselves, but no one stepped forward to speak to Elijah. The prophet shook his head in discouragement; the crowd would not give up the right to have two gods. Obadiah scrambled up to where Elijah stood and confirmed the unwillingness to stop worshiping Baal. The people were afraid of Ahab, he said. When Elijah climbed on a high rock and peered over at Ahab, he saw the king sitting comfortably among his servants with a smug expression on his face. Obviously Ahab thought Elijah had no chance of winning the people over to his side.

Once again Elijah stood before the people and began to speak. "I am the only one of the Lord's prophets here, but Baal has four hundred and fifty prophets. We have two fine bulls with us. Let the prophets of Baal choose one for themselves and prepare it for sacrifice but not set fire to it. I will prepare the other bull and put it on the wood but not set fire to it. They can call on Baal, and I will call on the name of the Lord. The god who answers—he is the true God. We will begin first thing in the morning."

This time the sound which arose from the

mountainside was more encouraging. Obadiah hurried down to walk among the people and find out what they were thinking. He ran back up to report breathlessly that Elijah's idea was being accepted. Ahab would have a fair chance to prove they should worship Baal, and Elijah would have a fair chance to prove his faith in God.

Elijah looked over at Ahab, who was marching around his camp shouting orders and threatening his prophets with punishment if they should fail and make him look foolish in front of all the people. His servants were already busying themselves with choosing the best bull and gathering wood for their sacrifice. In his usual confident manner, Elijah simply returned to his camp and laid out his bedroll. Once again Reuben was amazed at how calm the prophet remained. While his followers sat up late into the night talking about what might happen the next day,

THEY BUILT AN ALTAR FOR THEIR SACRIFICE.

"O BAAL, ANSWER US!"

Elijah slept soundly, undisturbed by their hushed conversation.

Elijah was awakened at dawn by the frantic noises coming from the top of the mountain. The prophets of Baal were directing servants to build an appropriate altar for this important sacrifice. The thousands of people on the mountainside crawled out of their tents and bedrolls to see enormous amounts of precious firewood being laid out carefully on the huge altar. As soon as the bull had been added to the heap, the prophets began pleading with Baal to answer their cry. "O Baal, answer us!" they shouted. Hundreds of prophets took turns standing near the altar and calling out aloud for Baal to strike fire to their sacrifice. The people from below crowded in as close as they could to see what was happening. When midmorning came and they still received no answer, the prophets began to dance around the altar.

"MAYBE HE IS SLEEPING
AND MUST BE AWAKENED."

Ahab watched from one side and hung his head in desperation. It seemed clear that Baal was not going to answer. Yet when the messengers came to ask if the prophets should continue calling on Baal, Ahab hastily insisted that they should not stop until their prayer was answered. Noontime came, and still nothing happened.

Elijah began to taunt the exhausted dancers. "Shout louder!" he said. "Surely he is a god! Perhaps he is deep in thought, or busy, or traveling. Maybe he is sleeping and must be awakened." Although they knew Elijah was ridiculing them, the prophets danced faster and shouted louder. One by one they began to slash themselves with swords and spears, hoping that their blood flow would arouse Baal to action.

By the middle of the afternoon, they were falling to the ground, their energy completely used up. They continued calling out to Baal even as they lay in the dirt with sweat running into their eyes. Still there was no answer.

The people were no longer watching with keen anticipation. Many thought that the prophets should admit their failure and give up rather than continue to humiliate themselves. They went about their evening meals almost unaware of the commotion which continued on the mountaintop. And then the news reached them that Elijah was beginning his sacrifice. Fleet-footed young men ran through the camps alerting every family of his actions.

Elijah and his small band of followers had begun dragging huge stones to the place where an altar to the Lord had fallen into ruins. Elijah explained that he would use twelve large stones to represent the twelve tribes of Israel so that the people would be reminded of the faith of their forefathers. He directed the servants to dig a wide

HE ARRANGED THE WOOD AND LAID THE BULL OUT.

trench around the altar as he arranged the wood and laid the bull out for sacrifice.

Finally he said to Obadiah and Reuben, "Fill four large jars with water and pour it on the offering and on the wood." The two young men were stunned by this request, yet they obeyed. Despite their earlier hesitations, they were convinced now that anything was possible when Elijah called upon the Lord. When they had drenched the altar, they returned to Elijah, who quietly told them to fill the four jars again and pour water on the altar. Once again they obeyed. After the daylong failure of Baal's prophets, onlookers were beginning to believe what Elijah said and were offering their water supply to be used to soak the altar. Elijah asked that the jugs be filled a third time. The water ran down around the altar and even filled the trench.

At last Elijah was satisfied that no could

accuse him of using tricks to start the fire. He stepped forward and began to pray in a loud voice: "O Lord, God of Abraham, Isaac and Israel, let it be known today that You are God in Israel and that I am Your servant and have done all these things at Your command. Answer me, O Lord, answer me, so these people will know that You, O Lord, are God, and that You are turning their hearts back again."

A stillness had come over the entire mountain. Night had fallen and the sky was pitch black. The paths were lit only by handheld candles, yet the people pressed in to see what would happen when Elijah prayed.

Abruptly the silence was cracked by a thunderous crash and the sky exploded with light from the altar. The roar of the flames could be heard even in Ahab's camp. In a matter of only a

THE SKY EXPLODED WITH LIGHT FROM THE ALTAR.

few minutes, the sacrifice was consumed, and the wood was turned to ashes. Even the water filling the trench was licked up by the intense heat.

The people immediately fell to the ground and stretched out and cried, "The Lord—He is God! We will worship God." The sound of the people praying was deafening as they wept and repented and promised a new allegiance to the true God. Only Ahab and the prophets of Baal did not bend their knees in worship.

Elijah himself began to weep with gratitude for the Lord's faithfulness and because now the people would turn their hearts back to God and defy Ahab and Jezebel. He looked over at the king's camp once again. Ahab knew that he had lost; his shoulders were slumped and his head hung low. He had accepted Elijah's challenge and had failed. The people would surely turn against him if he even threatened

"YOU WIN, ELIJAH!"

the prophet of the Lord.

Though hundreds of people were pressing in trying to get closer to him, Elijah gently pushed them aside and made his way slowly over to Ahab. He stood silently and waited for the king to speak.

"You win, Elijah," Ahab said spitefully.

"I do not seek victory, my king," Elijah said, humbly. "It is God who has proven true here tonight. Go and eat and drink as much as you like now, and listen for the sound of a heavy rain. The people will suffer no more."

8

PRAYING FOR RAIN

Elijah awoke early the next morning to the clanking of pots and pans being tied onto reluctant mules. Children were having one last slide in the dirt as their parents gathered their provisions and tied them into tight bundles for the trip down the mountain and across the countryside to their homes. Because of the long distance many of the people had to travel, their day had begun even before the sun had risen.

Looking in the direction of Ahab's camp, the prophet could sense the air of gloom which had fallen over the king's advisors and servants. At Elijah's insistence, the ancient law demanding the execution of prophets of pagan gods had been carried out. Eight hundred and fifty prophets of Baal and Asherah had been taken down the mountain the night before, leaving only about a hundred people still with Ahab. The king was in no hurry to leave Mount Carmel. Jezebel was waiting in Jezreel, halfway home to Samaria, and she would not be pleased with the way things had gone.

As the morning light seeped through the branches of the trees, Elijah decided that he must begin praying for rain. After all, this confrontation on Mount Carmel was supposed to prove that the Lord of Israel was the only true

God and bring an end to the drought and famine which had devastated the land for three years. He stood up and brushed off his clothes; he was still covered with ashes from the blaze the night before. After splashing some cold water on his face, he turned to climb a little higher and find a quiet place to be alone.

In a small clearing the weary prophet bent down to the ground and put his face between his knees to pray. "O Lord, true God of Israel and all the nations, You have heard the confession and repentance of the people. They have seen Your power and have turned their hearts back to You. The prophets of the false gods have been put to death according to Your holy law, and the people have pledged to worship only You. Holy and powerful God, now let it rain on the people. Send refreshment to the ground so that the animals may live and the

"O LORD, TRUE GOD OF ISRAEL. . ."

crops flourish and the people prosper."

Elijah remained in this position for several hours and continued to pray for heavy rains to fall upon the land. When he returned to his camp, he found Reuben and Obadiah and the others had awakened and begun to clean up some of the mess from the night before.

"Master!" Reuben called when he saw Elijah return. "The king has sent a messenger to ask when it will rain. He still does not believe what happened yesterday will make any difference for the drought. I did not know where you were, so I sent word back that God will provide the rain."

"You are right, Reuben." The prophet was obviously pleased with the faith that his servant now displayed. "And you will have an important role to play. I want you to climb around to the other side of the mountain and look out toward the sea. Come back and let me know if you see

"HE STILL DOES NOT BELIEVE WHAT HAPPENED
YESTERDAY WILL MAKE ANY DIFFERENCE."

THERE WAS ABSOLUTELY NO SIGN OF RAIN.

even the tiniest cloud or any sign of rain."

The young servant enthusiastically set out for the side of the mountain where he would be able to see the sea. Obadiah could not help himself and laughed aloud when he saw that Reuben was running too fast and had soon fallen flat on his face. Reuben ignored the teasing and was quickly up and running again, barely taking time to brush himself off. Elijah, who had hidden his own amusement at Reuben's misfortune, suggested that they all have something to eat while they waited for his return.

It seemed a long time before someone caught sight of Reuben heading back toward camp. He was not running this time; in fact, he seemed sluggish and discouraged. It was a cloudless day, he reported. He had stayed at his lookout point for several hours, hoping to see a cloud waft across the sky, but there had been nothing.

There was absolutely no sign of rain.

The men gathered around to hear Reuben's report exchanged glances with each other, but none of them dared to look directly at Elijah. Was it possible he was wrong about the rain? they wondered. If it were really going to rain, surely there would be clouds over the sea. No one spoke. The only sound was someone shuffling his foot around in the dirt.

Finally Elijah said, "Go again, Reuben," and turned and walked away.

Reuben looked questioningly at Obadiah, who shrugged his shoulders. Choosing his footholds more carefully this time, Reuben retraced the path around the mountain to his lookout point. While he was gone, the camp was silent except for an occasional cough or someone shifting his position. Though he did not speak, it did not seem that Elijah had lost confidence. From time to time, the men would see that his head was bowed and he was praying again, and they would soundlessly bow their own heads also.

By the time Reuben returned, it was the middle of the day. As the group looked at him expectantly in the distance, he began to shake his head to let them know he had seen no clouds. Elijah kept to himself as the others gathered around Reuben to speculate on what was happening. Perhaps the rain would come tomorrow or next week, someone suggested, and Elijah would be just as right. Wasn't it enough that the people had repented? Did they have to have rain the very next day? Or perhaps Elijah should go back up the mountainside himself to pray again. They spoke softly so that Elijah would not hear the doubt in their voices.

They were abruptly interrupted by a servant from Ahab's camp who was approaching Elijah.

ELIJAH KEPT TO HIMSELF.

Reuben rushed over to block the boy's way, but Elijah signaled that he would speak to him. As everyone expected, Ahab again wanted to know about the rain. His taunting message implied that Elijah's prayers were weak and that his God would not answer. The prophet curtly sent the boy back with no answer for Ahab and turned to Reuben once again.

"Go once more, Reuben. There will be rain! There must be rain!"

"I will go also," Obadiah said. Ahab's mocking message had rallied the energy of the whole group, and they were once again intent on proving to Ahab the power of the true God.

The two friends had not been gone long when they were seen returning to camp. Because they had returned so soon, the rumor spread that they had seen rain clouds. They hastily denied this, reporting once again that there had been no sign of rain. However, they had returned for their bedrolls and a few supplies; they would spend the night keeping watch and return in the morning with their news.

The main camp sat up very late talking around the fire. One by one they drifted off to sleep, but Elijah sat up alone. *Why,* he wondered, *after God demonstrated His power on Mount Carmel in such an undeniable way—why is there no rain?* The air around him was completely dry and absolutely still without the slightest hint of a breeze. It was a long night of torturous blackness for Elijah.

Reuben and Obadiah returned early in the morning. They moved quietly around the camp as the others, except Elijah, slept. As he prepared breakfast, Reuben noticed the bags under Elijah's eyes and guessed that he had been sitting up all night. The prophet accepted his

WHY? HE WONDERED.

morning bread cakes in silence but did little more than nibble at the edges.

"Master," Reuben finally said, "I will go a fifth time. Whenever I have questioned the wisdom of your actions, you have always reminded me that you are the Lord's servant and you do what He commands. I believe He has told you there will be rain. I will go again to the sea."

Reuben was gone before most of the others woke up. As the morning passed, a few made preparations for the journey home. The rain would come or the rain would not come, they reasoned. It did not matter whether they waited with Elijah or returned home to their families. As Elijah looked over the mountainside, he could see that it was nearly empty. The people had left to resume their normal routines. However, Ahab's camp was still firmly established, standing as a visible reminder of the challenge which remained unresolved.

Tired and dusty, Reuben returned for the midday meal still shaking his head. It had now been two days since the Lord had struck fire to the sacrifice and still there was no sign of rain. After briefly refreshing himself with food and water, he set out again, his steps noticeably slower than the day before.

With little to keep them occupied while they waited, the remaining men stretched out to rest. The bright sun warmed them and made them sleepy, and soon most of them had dozed off. Elijah continued to sit alone and pray, confident that the Lord would send rain but wondering why he had not yet done so.

Suddenly Obadiah jumped up and shouted, "Here comes Reuben! He's running! It must be good news!"

Breathlessly, Reuben reported that he had at

REUBEN RETURNED, STILL SHAKING HIS HEAD.

last seen a very small cloud hanging over the sea. At first he was not sure, but he looked again and was positive. It was as small as his hand, but it was definitely a rain cloud. Obadiah and several others immediately ran off on the path which Reuben had beaten down with his seven trips to the sea. They were anxious to see for themselves what Reuben had seen.

Elijah leaned back against a large rock and sighed heavily. He did not need to see for himself; he knew there would be rain and very soon. He motioned to Reuben that he had one last task for the servant; he was to go tell Ahab to hitch up his chariot and leave the mountain, because a heavy rain was coming. This was a message Reuben was glad to carry, and he immediately dashed off to do his master's bidding.

The sky was already becoming dark, and in only a few minutes, it was as black as night.

Elijah's followers were scurrying around camp, rapidly covering their supplies to protect them from the rain. Gusty winds were blowing over their tents, and some of the smaller men had difficulty even standing up against the violent movement of air. Rain began to pour down in thick, heavy sheets, turning the dry mountainside to mud and pushing the soil down toward the valley.

Elijah saw that Ahab had taken his advice and tried to leave before the rains began. Despite the rising mud, his chariot was making good progress toward the valley. The thunder was deafening as it rattled the sky, and the lightning was the only light that shattered the darkness of the day. Although he knew he was not a young man and Ahab was well ahead of him in a chariot pulled by horses, Elijah felt a strange power surging through his muscles. Following the commands of the voiceless pressure inside his head, he

RAIN BEGAN TO POUR DOWN!

tucked his garment up around his belt and began running. He ran so fast that he passed Ahab.

Ahab shouted furiously and angrily as he realized that the Lord's prophet was ahead of him and the Lord's thundercloud was behind him. Once again he had been humiliated by that silly old man!

9

Visit from an Angel

It was with great reluctance that Ahab drove his chariot into the streets of Jezreel and returned to the place where he knew Jezebel would be waiting for him. *That woman will nag me to death one day*, he thought to himself sorrowfully.

Jezebel was indeed furious. Through the families passing through Jezreel on their journeys home, the news of Elijah's victory on Mount Carmel had reached her before Ahab's arrival.

THEY MADE FUN OF THE PROPHETS OF BAAL.

Thousands of people had been to the mountain and seen what happened, so there could be no doubting that it was true. The streets were buzzing with excitement. Shopkeepers met in the streets to tell the story again as women and little children gathered around them to hear. Older children danced wildly in the streets as they made fun of the prophets of Baal who had danced at the altar before their silent god. Jezebel looked on, seething with anger.

As soon as Ahab walked through the door of their temporary headquarters, she screamed at him. "How could you let this happen? You are the king of Israel and he is nothing!"

Ahab's shoulder's sagged as he sat down wearily. He was too exhausted to argue with Jezebel, and he wished she would just go away. But he knew she would not.

"I am ashamed at the weakling you have

"HOW COULD YOU LET THIS HAPPEN?"

become," she continued, shrieking at the top of her voice. "I told you to kill him three years ago and again when he came to you with this ridiculous challenge. But you did not listen to me. No, you allowed him to humiliate you over and over again."

The king was worn out and could only sigh in disgust at her accusations. "You weren't there, Jezebel. You don't know what it was like."

"Do I have to go everywhere with you just to keep you out of trouble? Can't you do anything for yourself?" The longer she spoke, the more shrill her voice became.

"If I had turned down his challenge on the road that day, I would have humiliated myself in front of my entire staff."

"You should have killed him!" she screeched.

"I can't just lop off the head of someone as popular as Elijah! Why can't you understand that? The people would revolt." After his grueling experience on the mountain, Ahab was in no mood for this discussion with Jezebel, but he continued. "You might as well know, all the prophets of Baal have been executed."

"What! Why would you order such a thing?"

"I didn't order it. Elijah did."

"Elijah is not king; you are."

"He claimed to be following the Law of Moses. My advisors agreed that their execution was demanded by Israel's law."

"When did you start paying attention to the Law of Moses? Surely you could have stopped it."

Ahab had never seen Jezebel as full of rage as she was at that moment. He had been chiding himself for two days because of his lack of control over the events on the mountain, and now his own wife was ready to send him to the executioner as well. He had no answer for her.

"I WILL SEE TO IT THAT ELIJAH IS STOPPED!"

"I can see that once again I will have to take matters into my own hands. I will see to it that Elijah is stopped!" Jezebel signaled to her frightened servant to follow and marched out of the room.

Elijah had reached Jezreel ahead of Ahab and had seen him pass by. He was not surprised when the messenger from the king's household came looking for him and told him of Jezebel's wrath. Her message was short and direct: "May the gods deal with me, be it ever so severely, if by this time tomorrow I do not make your life like that of one of them." Obviously the death of the prophets of Baal was intolerable to Jezebel. When the messenger had gone, Reuben and Elijah turned to look at each other.

"Master," Reuben began, "she is really angry this time. I think this is a real threat to your life! This is not like the times when she has mocked

"I HAVE BEEN WANTING TO GO TO HOREB."

Ahab for allowing you to live."

Elijah sighed heavily. "I'm afraid you are right, my friend. She is still calling on nonexistent gods. She has learned nothing from what happened on Mount Carmel. We dare not even spend the night here. Gather our things together immediately while I explain to Obadiah and the others that we must leave."

"Where will we go, Master?" the servant asked, wondering where they could go to escape Jezebel's anger.

"I have been wanting to go to Horeb, where God's covenant with Moses was first established."

"That is a very long way from here, Master."

"Yes, but I think I should go. If we travel at night and keep moving quickly, perhaps we can get out of Jezebel's reach."

Reuben could see that the prophet was very upset at Jezebel's threat and quickly bundled up

"THIS IS WHERE WE PART, MY FRIEND."

their belongings. They stayed hidden in the crowded streets until they were safely at the edge of town, and then they began the long journey south toward the desert.

Wherever they traveled, Elijah was recognized and people were anxious to help them. They were given food and clean, dry beds to refresh themselves after walking in the rain that continued to pour down. As the days passed, they made good progress and began to feel that probably Jezebel no longer was on their trail. But they dared not return north. More and more Elijah preferred to push on in silence, and his steps grew slower every day. Reuben made the best meals he could with the provisions they had and tried to make Elijah as comfortable as possible when they slept, but he knew his master was growing more discouraged every day.

When they reached Beersheeba, Elijah said

to Reuben, "This is where we part, my friend."

Reuben was shocked. They had been together for such a long time—why would Elijah want to leave him now? "Master!" he cried.

"Reuben, I'm going on alone from here. I am worn-out and discouraged, and I feel so frazzled that I can't think straight."

"But you wanted to go to Mount Horeb, and we are still a long way from there. I want to be with you, to look after you."

"I appreciate that, Reuben, and we will be together again, I promise. But I must be alone right now."

Elijah left his dismayed servant and traveled on for another full day into the desert. The rains had ceased and the sun was hot. There was no visible road in the desert, and no one else was in sight. Finally he collapsed under a broom tree, the only shrubbery he had found all day, and

"I HAVE HAD ENOUGH, LORD."

there he poured out his bitter heart to God. "I have had enough, Lord," he said. "Take my life. My work has been fruitless; there is no point in living." Too exhausted even to pray, he dropped back against the tree and fell into a deep sleep.

All at once he felt someone touching his shoulder. Thinking it was a dream, he tried to shrug off the feeling, but it grew stronger. When he opened his eyes, he saw an angel standing before him. Still not sure if he was dreaming or not, he said nothing. The angel pointed to a steaming bread cake and a jug of water. "Get up and eat," he said. Without understanding what was happening, Elijah obediently ate the food before him and then lay down again.

Once more he was awakened. The angel said, "Get up and eat, for the journey is too much for you." Elijah was more alert this time. Somehow the angel knew that he wanted to travel the

HE SAW AN ANGEL STANDING BEFORE HIM.

long distance to Horeb but did not have the strength to get there. There were more bread cakes and water waiting for him. He filled up until he could eat no more and then set out on his journey once again.

For forty long days and nights, Elijah traveled through the desert. Although he did not encounter anyone along the way, he never lacked food or water. In his mind he knew that God was caring for him and had not abandoned him. In his heart, however, he was overwhelmed with discouragement and despaired of continuing to live the life of a prophet.

At last he came to Horeb. Looking around the isolated mountain in the middle of the desert, he found a small cave. He wrapped his tattered blanket around his tired form and crawled in, hoping to find the relief that only sleep would bring.

10

WIND AND FIRE

Elijah slept fitfully that night. He was completely exhausted from his months of running from Jezebel, and though the Lord had faithfully provided for his physical needs as he journeyed, he was unable to shake the dejection which gripped his soul. He huddled in the cave without even a candle and wondered again why the Lord would not permit him to die and be released from this misery.

"What are you doing here, Elijah?" Elijah jumped in the darkness as the strange, strong voice echoed in the cave. Then he held perfectly still and peered into the blackness around him, looking for the source of the words and wondering who would know he was there. "What are you doing here, Elijah?" the voice repeated, and Elijah knew that it was the Lord speaking to him. He had become accustomed over the years to hearing a whisper inside his head when the Lord was leading him, but never had he heard anything like this.

Although he felt foolish talking out loud alone in the dark, Elijah answered, "I have been very zealous for the Lord God Almighty. The Israelites have rejected your covenant, broken down your altars, and put Your prophets to death with the sword. Even after what happened on

Mount Carmel, I am being chased and must run for my life. I am the only prophet left, and now they are trying to kill me, too."

There was a long silence, and Elijah began to wonder if he was imagining the entire conversation. The voice spoke at last. "Go out and stand on the mountain in the presence of the Lord, for the Lord is about to pass by."

The prophet was still not sure what was really happening, but he obeyed. Shaking off the worn-out blanket wrapped around him, he crawled out of the cave and into the early morning light. He climbed higher and higher until he reached the top of the mountain and waited there. What had the voice meant when it said that the presence of the Lord was about to pass by? he wondered. *How will I know for sure when it happens?*

Suddenly, the air, which had been still all day,

HE FELT THE ENTIRE MOUNTAIN SHUDDER!

began to whirl around him. Elijah covered his face with his arms to keep the dirt and sand away. Under his feet he felt the entire mountain shudder helplessly against the force of the powerful, ripping wind. He heard a rumbling above his head and looked up just in time to see an avalanche roaring down the mountainside directly at him. Frightened and with his heart beating very hard, Elijah ran as fast as he could out of its path. He saw the rocks shatter into pieces as they flew by him.

As suddenly as it began, it was all over. The evidence was all around him: broken rocks, uprooted trees, gaping holes in the side of the mountain. Elijah was left with the sound of his own heavy breathing and made an effort to calm down. The chaos had stopped; he was safe now, he thought. Had that been the Lord passing by? Elijah realized that in the midst of that dramatic

ELIJAH WAS THROWN OFF THE ROCK.

display of power, he had felt only a cold void and not the familiar comfort of the Lord. He sat down on a large piece of a shattered boulder and tried to make his heart stop beating so fast.

It was then that he felt the shaking of the ground underneath him. The earth vibrated with such force that Elijah was thrown off the rock and found himself rolling down the mountain. Opening up before him was a deep crevice as the earth cracked and the great mountain shifted on its foundation. Never had Elijah experienced an earthquake of such force. Now he was truly frightened—first the wind, now this! And still he did not feel the presence of the Lord. When the Lord himself did pass at last, would it completely destroy the mountain?

Elijah had many questions but no time to ask them. He reached out and grabbed a piece of shrubbery to keep himself from plunging into the newly-formed ravine. After a few moments, when he was sure the earth had stopped moving, he stood up and brushed himself off. All at once the very bush he had used to save himself burst into flames. Elijah immediately bolted out of range of the fire, only to find that every bush around him was blazing. He scrambled down the mountain toward the cave, more afraid of losing his life now than in all the months of running from Jezebel. He felt further than ever from the presence of the Lord.

From the refuge of the cave, Elijah watched the fire consume everything in its path and then burn itself out as suddenly as it had begun. He stood absolutely still as ashes gently floated in the air and settled on the ground. The mountain had returned to its silent state, and Elijah stood motionless waiting for whatever might come next. The wind, earthquake, and fire had

EVERY BUSH AROUND HIM WAS BLAZING.

demonstrated God's mighty power, but still Elijah had not seen the presence of the Lord pass by the mountain.

And then he heard it. At first he thought it might be just branches rubbing in the breeze or the last lick of flames being smothered in the dirt. The voice was speaking again—not thunderously as before, but gently and quietly, really just a whisper. "Elijah, what are you doing here?" The Lord asked the same question once again.

The frustrated prophet did not know how to answer. *If God will judge the people with the wind, earthquake, and fire He has just shown, then my work will mean something,* he thought to himself. Elijah was convinced that as long as Ahab and Jezebel were in power, there would be no permanent change in the people. Was God telling him that he had to go back and continue in his fruitless effort? Elijah was reluctant to accept this, so he gave the same answer he had given before.

"I have been very zealous for the Lord God Almighty. The Israelites have rejected Your covenant, broken down Your altars, and put Your prophets to death with this sword. I am the only one left, and now they are trying to kill me, too."

Even as he spoke them, Elijah knew his words were hollow. For a moment the Lord said nothing. During the silence Elijah realized his own need for the presence of the Lord, as well as the nation's need to return to the Lord. God had not abandoned him but had met him on Mount Horeb and demonstrated that the Lord was not powerless. God had spoken to him in a gentle, encouraging whisper.

"What am I doing here?" he asked aloud. Clearly his work was not finished. There was much more to do.

ELIJAH KNEW HIS WORDS WERE HOLLOW.

The gentle voice whispered again in his ear. "Go back the way you came, and go to the Desert of Damascus. When you get there, anoint Hazael king over Aram. Also anoint Jehu son of the Nimshi king over Israel, and anoint Elisha son of Shaphat from Abel Meholah to succeed you as prophet. Jehu will put to death any who escape the sword of Hazael, and Elisha will put to death any who escape the sword of Jehu. I reserve seven thousand in Israel—all whose knees have not bowed down to Baal and whose mouths have not kissed him."

And then the voice was gone. Elijah listened for a long time for more, but there was only the sound of the wind and the rustling leaves. But enough had been said. Elijah stood with his cloak wrapped tightly around him and tried to absorb what he had been told. He had thought that his work was over, that Israel was lost to

HE WOULD BE PART OF THE EVENTS.

Baal and that he alone believed in God. Now he knew that God had not given up on Israel and that many exciting things were about to happen—and he would be part of the events, along with thousands of other people who had not bowed down to Baal.

No longer tired, the prophet started his descent down the mountain and wondered where he should start looking for Reuben after so much time had passed.

11

ELISHA

Reuben was overjoyed to see his beloved master return from weeks in the desert. Elijah was refreshed and full of energy and now walked so fast that Reuben had trouble keeping up. Damascus, where the Lord had told him to go, was hundreds of miles north of Mount Horeb, and the prophet was anxious to continue the work of God. Over and over again, Reuben asked Elijah to tell him the stories of the angel under the broom tree and of the wind, earthquake, and fire on the mountain. Most of all, he wanted to hear how Elijah had heard God speak aloud in a quiet, gentle voice. Each time that he told the stories to Reuben, Elijah understood better that the Lord was in control and still had a great deal of work for him to do. Many weeks passed in pleasant companionship as the two friends made their way east and north toward Damascus.

At last the day arrived that they stood at the edge of a large field and watched a robust young man plowing. His muscles rippled as he effortlessly guided the oxen to do their work. Twenty-four oxen yoked together in pairs submitted to his commands and pulled the enormous plow as it dug deeply into the black earth. Shafts of iron glinted in the sun as they rotated into the ground

ELIJAH WAS SURE THAT THIS WAS ELISHA.

and back up again. The young man, darkly tanned from years in the sun, was obviously used to working very hard. Elijah was sure that this was Elisha, the man who would continue the work of a prophet after he himself was gone.

Reuben was surprised when his master called out the young man's name. Elisha was also surprised; how did these strangers know who he was? He could not explain the feeling, but he was drawn to the older man and was eager to begin a conversation with him—especially after he found out that this was the famous prophet Elijah standing in his field. The three sat in the shade of a tree, and a servant brought a light meal to them. As the afternoon waned, Elijah took his personal cloak and threw it around Elisha's shoulders. It was a very serious moment; both men knew that this meant Elisha would become a prophet and walk in Elijah's footsteps.

ELIJAH THREW HIS CLOAK
AROUND ELISHA'S SHOULDERS.

When it was time for Elijah to leave, Elisha jumped up in protest. "Please," he said, "let me go with you now. I will say good-bye to my family and join your work." Instinctively, Elisha knew that he would never return to the work of the plow. He ordered his servants to slaughter the twelve teams of oxen and then burn the huge plow to cook the meat. That evening, he held a great feast and gave the freshly cooked meat to many people who needed it. Then he said farewell to his family and sought out Elijah, resolved to travel with him and learn from him as much as possible.

The two prophets traveled together for several years after that. Ahab and Jezebel continued to be an evil influence over the people of Israel, but Elijah had little direct contact with them—until news reached him about Naboth's vineyard.

In their travels, the prophets had seen Naboth's vineyard; Elisha recognized it as rich, productive land which any farmer would want to have, and Naboth did an excellent joy getting a good crop. Elijah learned that Ahab had offered to buy the land, but Naboth did not want to sell. Sullen and angry, the king had gone home to pout. He was extremely frustrated and did not even want to eat. Jezebel, as always, reminded him he was the king, and he could have anything he wanted. In fact, she promised to get the land for him herself. Once again, she shook her head at Ahab's weakness and took control of the situation.

The queen wrote letters to important people in the city where Naboth lived and pretended the king had written them. Following her instructions, the leaders held a feast to honor Naboth but arranged for two scoundrels to come and tell

THE KING HAD GONE HOME TO POUT.

lies about him. They said that he had cursed both God and the king and ought to be stoned to death. When the messenger brought word that everything had gone just as Jezebel had planned, she smiled smugly and went to tell Ahab the news. Soon the king had possession of the valuable land.

This is when Elijah and Elisha went to see King Ahab. Elisha watched in awe as Elijah stood up to the king and spoke the word of the Lord. For many years after, he remembered the old man's bravery when he spoke judgment against the king for stealing Naboth's land. Elijah said boldly, "Have you not murdered a man and seized his property? Just as the dogs licked up Naboth's blood, they will lick up yours!"

When Ahab realized that he had been tricked by Jezebel, he cried out in anger. He had done many evil things during his years as king,

AHAB REALIZED HOW WRONG HE HAD BEEN.

and many of them had been suggested by Jezebel. Now she had taken advantage of him and made him responsible for a horrible deed he had not wanted to do.

After a lifetime of disobedience to the Lord and many years of threatening Elijah, suddenly Ahab realized how wrong he had been to pay attention to Jezebel for so long. He stood before the prophets and tore his clothes and declared that he would fast to demonstrate his repentance to the Lord. Elijah and Ahab had been enemies for so long that now the prophet could hardly believe the change in Ahab. But the king seemed genuinely sorry for the way he had been living and truly humble. He no longer challenged Elijah's authority, and his servants and advisors could hardly believe this was the same man. Jezebel, of course, thought he had completely lost his mind.

HIS OWN TIME ON EARTH WOULD SOON BE OVER.

It was three years later when word reached Elijah that Ahab had been killed in battle while trying to regain land taken by the king of Aram several years earlier. Despite the many years they had spent on opposite sides of God's law, Elijah was sorry that Ahab had met his death in such a violent way. He also knew that this meant that his own time on earth would soon be over. There would be a new king, and it would be Elisha who would declare the word of God throughout the land from now on.

12

CHARIOT OF FIRE

"This is where Reuben and I were fed by ravens," Elijah said, pointing in the direction of the ravine where they had taken refuge many years earlier. "I'll never forget the look on Reuben's face the first time the birds came and brought us food."

Reuben smiled as he too remembered the sweet time they had enjoyed together during those weeks. He told Elisha, "That was right after Elijah faced Ahab and predicted a famine if he did not repent."

"If only he had repented sooner than he did," Elisha said, and the others nodded in agreement.

Reuben and Elijah went on to tell Elisha the whole story of that encounter with the king, and of course Elisha remembered how the drought and famine had affected his own family's farm. By now Elisha knew almost everything that had happened during Elijah's years of working for the Lord; but every time he heard the stories repeated, he was again reminded of how powerful and compassionate God was. He prayed that he would have as deep a relationship with God as the older prophet had.

"Why don't the two of you stay here and rest a while?" Elijah said. "The Lord is calling me to Bethel."

Elisha protested immediately. "As surely as

THE THREE OF THEM WALKED
THE FEW MILES TO BETHEL.

the Lord lives and as you live, I will not leave you." Reuben, of course, also did not want to leave his master, so the three of them walked the few miles to Bethel.

When they arrived at Bethel, Elijah led the way through the streets to where a group of prophets would be meeting. Although they were expecting Elijah, they were surprised to see Elisha. "Elisha, do you know that the Lord is going to take your master from you today?"

"Yes, I know," Elisha said, for he, too, had heard the voice of God that morning. "But let's not talk about it."

The group knew that this would be their last meeting with Elijah, and they felt a mixture of sadness at his absence and happiness about what they knew was going to happen to him. At last Elijah said that he must move on to Jericho, and they said their tearful farewells.

"THE LORD IS GOING TO TAKE
YOUR MASTER FROM YOU TODAY."

Again Elijah invited Elisha to stay behind, but the younger prophet insisted on continuing on. The prophets in Jericho were just as surprised to see him as those in Bethel had been, and they asked the same question: "Do you know that the Lord is going to take your master from you today?"

Elisha tried hard to keep his voice steady as he said, "Yes, but let's not talk about it."

After saying good-bye to these friends, the travelers moved on once again, going to the Jordan River. Again Elisha refused to stay behind. When they approached the river, they realized that the group from Jericho had also not stayed behind. There were fifty men following behind them but keeping their distance. Without speaking to Elijah, they stopped at a point where they would be able to see the marvelous event which would soon take place.

"Master," Reuben said, "the boat is further down. How are we going to cross the river at this spot?"

Elijah did not respond. He silently removed his cloak and rolled it up till it was tight and thick. Then he held it by both hands and lifted his arms high above his head. He swung down heavily, and the cloak slapped the water hard. Immediately the water rolled back in both directions, and a path of dry ground appeared. Elisha had never before seen the prophet display such power and was at first startled by what he saw. He knew, however, that this was Elijah's last act on earth.

When they had crossed the river, Elijah turned to Reuben and said, "My friend, what would I have done without you all these years?"

Reuben could not speak, but he tried to smile at his master who was also his best friend.

HE LIFTED HIS ARMS HIGH ABOVE HIS HEAD.

Then Elijah pulled Elisha to him and wrapped his arms around the young man. "Tell me, what can I do for you before I am taken from you?"

"Let me carry on your work," Elisha whispered emotionally.

"The Lord told me to anoint you as my successor, and now it is in His hands. If you see me when I am taken, then the work will be yours—otherwise not."

They walked along and talked some more about the work that still needed to be done, knowing that at any moment something very dramatic might happen, or Elijah might simply disappear very quietly. Suddenly a chariot and horses made of fire appeared on the road and roared past them. Before they could even make sense out of what they were seeing, the two prophets were sheared apart. The roaring continued

ELIJAH HAD BEEN LIFTED TO THE SKY!

even though the chariot of fire was out of sight, and Elisha realized it was the sound of a powerful rushing whirlwind. Looking up he saw that Elijah had been lifted to the sky in a twirling air which had touched nothing else around him. The clouds parted, and Elijah was gone from his sight.

Elisha stood motionless for a long time with his eyes lifted upward. The clouds had resumed their normal formation and floated white and puffy against the blue sky. The sun was shining brilliantly, and anyone standing on the bank of the Jordan would have thought it was an ordinary day.

But it was not an ordinary day, not for Elijah and not for Elisha. When at last he lowered his eyes, Elisha saw his teacher's cloak, still wet from smacking the river, lying at his feet. He picked it up and turned back to the Jordan.

No, this was no ordinary day.

YOUNG READER'S CHRISTIAN LIBRARY

Be sure to check out other books in this series!

Written just for readers
ages 8 to 12, these stories
really come to life with
dozens of illustrations. Kids
will learn about the people,
events, and ideas that had a
tremendous impact on
Christian history.

Paperback, 192 pages each

ONLY
$1.49 EACH!

Elijah	Esther
Jesus	Eric Liddell
Abraham Lincoln	Lydia
Samuel Morris	Florence Nightingale
Paul	The Pilgrim's Progress
Ruth	Sojourner Truth

Available wherever Christian books are sold.